ARTHUR DOBRIN
MANUEL CORTIZO, Photographer

Spiritual Timber

Reflections to help build a life of compassion and justice

© 2020 Arthur Dobrin

Photography: © Manuel Cortizo, except the photographs on pages 16, 37, 48, 52 and 59 that belong to Lyn Dobrin's private archive.

Design and layout: Alicia Hermida

"Spiritual Timber" by Arthur Dobrin.
 ISBN 978-0-9963718-1-0

Published by American Ethical Union © 2020. All rights reserved.

Manufactured in the United States of America.

Open your ears, there is beauty to be heard.
Open your eyes, there is beauty to be seen.
Open your heart, there is beauty to be felt.

Index

Preface

This collection of my epigrams addresses life's yearning to find fulfillment and happiness. At its heart is the belief that all rational people want to overcome alienation and separation and desire to live a life of acceptance and purpose. This goal, I believe, is achievable through self- cultivation. Properly understood, self-cultivation involves developing habits and attitudes that lead to ethical relationships. Joy and happiness result from living properly as part of the human community and natural world. My religious tradition calls this ethical culture. It recognizes that when we are not in harmony with others, when we separate ourselves from the world around us, when we use others, when we disregard and disrespect others, when we treat others unjustly we become sick in our hearts. For it is the ethical life — a life of goodness — that allows us to prosper. That is, living compassionately is living happily. Living justly is life fulfilled. Living with equanimity is a life of inner peace.

Many traditions set a time to reflect on deep matters. Some call it prayer, others meditation. It is a period for assessing values and behaviors to make them more consistent with our highest aspirations. It is a time for re-generation and renewal. It is a time to ensure that the ties that bind haven't been unwittingly broken or, if they have, learning how to mend the break and providing the inner strength to put things right.

Many years ago I began to think about what makes life sweet and what makes it bitter. My own experiences as a humanist minister for more than three decades and as a teacher of applied ethics with undergraduate students at the university have taught me that there is a core of wisdom found throughout the world that points in the same direction.

From the richness of philosophies and religions, I've synthesized these thoughts into what I think of as spiritual timber. Here is material with which to construct a home, one with air and light, shutters thrown open and doors ajar. It is a home of shelter, protection and warmth. This is the material to make an inviting and expansive home, one that welcomes the world in. This is a home of generosity and respect, peace and hospitality.

This collection is modeled upon those religious and philosophical traditions that present their views not through argument or theory only but also in brief forms, succinctly, sometimes plainly, sometimes metaphorically. In a manner this is a breviary, to be used in whatever way you find useful. I think it is most helpful when read in sections, not as a whole, and to be treated as something to be returned to and understood in the light of new experiences.

There is no Map

"I have a map that leads to the world's great treasure," someone once said.

The neighbor saw the map and killed the owner. He then took the map, read it carefully, and set out to find the treasure.

Not long after, he reached the place marked on the map and there, just as had been promised, he found diamonds and gold. The person sat upon the glittering treasure at first full of happiness. But when he died years later, he was full of sorrow and regret.

"I have a map that leads to the world's great treasure," someone once said to her neighbor.

"How much do you want for it?" the neighbor asked.

"It is yours without charge," she said. "All I srequest is that you take me along with you."

The neighbor grabbed the map and ran away as fast as she could. She then carefully looked at the marks upon the paper and followed them step-by-step until she found the treasure, just as had been promised. She rested now and admired the glittering jewels. She sat upon the glittering treasure at first full of happiness. But when she died years later, she was full of sorrow and regret.

"I have a map that leads you to the world's great treasure," someone said to his neighbor.

"What do I have to do to see this map?" the neighbor asked. "Take me along with you," the owner said.

So the neighbor did. They two studied the map together, discussing which way to go and what they would need along the way. They often disagreed about the direction and they argued about the provisions to bring. Then, they began their journey.

When they came to a fork in the road, they studied the map again. Sometimes they raised their voices in disagreement and argued about which turn to take. They sought directions. Finally, they settled on a path and continued on their way. They argued about many things, discussed what to do and how to do it. They disagreed and sought advice. There were times they were so angry they didn't talk to one another for a day or two. In fact, they never completely agreed with each other. But they always tried to understand one another. So they talked, remained silent, thought and talked some more and finally found a way to move on. Always they walked together, first one in the lead, then the other, then side-by-side.

The neighbors picked fruits and nuts from the trees and found clean water. They repaired the tears in their clothes. They built shelter and found fuel to keep warm. One knew the stars, so they could travel from place to place; the other knew all the plants that grew, so they could reap the bounty of the earth. One sang old songs and one made-up new ones. One loved the beauty of numbers, the other the beauty of words. One drew picture, and one tried making new things.

Finally they stopped wandering and stayed put.

"This is delicious," they said, as they spiced and salted their food.

"This is beautiful," they said, as they admired the flowers on their table.

Every once in awhile they took out their map and wondered.

Eventually the map yellowed and became fragile from many folds. It grew brittle and the markings faded until they were barely visible to any eye.

First one died, then the other. They had been full of sorrow in losing one another, but they had no regrets. They were only full of gratitude for having lived such a life.

There is no map
for the great treasure

Towards Happiness

- Life's true treasures are always at hand.

- Life's true treasures never belong to you alone.

- I can sing alone.
  But sing with me and make me happy once again.

- Life's true treasures can never be held in the hand alone.
  They must also be held in the heart.

- Life's true treasures can never be held in the hand or heart alone.
  They must not be held at all.

- When you are grateful, you will know happiness,
  As you will see the fullness that you already have.

- When you express your gratitude,
  you will bring joy to others' lives.
  When others know joy,
  your life will be filled with happiness.

- The places of happiness are infinite,
  the sources never ending.
  You inhabit those places
  because you have let them in.

- How do you know when you have achieved happiness?
  There will be a sense of inner peace.

The Important Things

- These are the important things in life:
  Cultivating a good heart.
  Cultivating a good mind.
  Cultivating good deeds.

- The unimportant things are used and
  then used up.
  The important things are used
  but never used up.

- When the heart, mind and
  deeds are right you are good.

- When two hearts are in tune, the universe sings.

- A heart never in tune causes
  the universe to tremble.

- A happy heart is a shared heart.

- An educated heart is a generous heart.

- An empty heart rattles.
  It is the noise of the self in love with itself.

- When heart, mind and deed harmonize,
  the world becomes good. In a good world,
  everyone can be happy.

True Happiness

- It is your duty to create a world of happiness.

- Here are the things that lead to a happy life:
  Study someone whose life is happy.
  Find a teacher whose values you admire.
  Have a child in your life.
  Associate with people whose judgments you trust,
  Look to people whose lives serve as an inspiration.
  Make small the gap between what
  you say and what you do.

- There is no happiness without harmony.
  There is no harmony without respect.
  Therefore, respect others and you will find happiness.

- There is no happiness without justice.
  Therefore, if you want to be happy, act justly.

- Begrudging others leads to disharmony.
  Without harmony there can be no happiness.
  Therefore, let go of grudges and restore harmony.
  In a harmonious world, happiness is possible.

- Happiness at another's expense is an offence
  against the community. To offend the community
  is to be self-centered.
  That which is self-centered is short-lived.

- Receiving gifts graciously is a gift to the giver.
  Graciousness is a gift of the heart.
  A gift of the heart is a gift of happiness.

- Gifts properly given bring happiness to giver and receiver alike. Gifts improperly given create resentment and shame.
  Therefore, be thoughtful and careful in what and how you give.

- Others become happy when you show them appreciation.

- Being cherished is a source of supreme happiness.

- You are most happy when you act upon compassionate feelings.

- When your heart has been opened happiness is infinite.

Compassionate Living

- You are part of society.
  Therefore, happiness is created through
  compassionate living.

- Compassion is part of human nature.
  Cultivate the compassionate part of yourself and
  connect to others.

- Reason is part of human nature.
  Cultivate the reasonable part of yourself
  so you make sound decisions.

- Compassion is part of human nature.
  Reason is part of human nature.
  Therefore, make no separation between heart and mind.
  Emotion and reason, feeling and thought —
  all that is human.

- Compassion and thoughtfulness lead to good deeds.

- You realize your own humanity in compassion and justice.

- A corrupt heart rattles with greed.

- You may reside in another's heart even at a distance.
  The greater reward is hearts in close contact.

- If your heart is acquisitive,
  you will lead a life of disappointment.
  If your heart is generous, your life will be satisfied.

- A closed fist can't offer a helping hand.
  A closed heart can't find fellow-feeling.

- Listen with an open mind.
  Listen with an open heart.
  Let the other in.
  This is the way of respect.

- You cannot know peace if your heart
  if full of bitterness.

- A heart full of fear cannot feel
  its own compassion.

Living in Troubled Times

- To live without fear is to live in fortunate times.
  Fortunate times, like comets, are rare events.
  Therefore, fear is commonplace.

- Every sentient creature knows fear.
  Therefore, you are not alone in the fear that you feel.

- To know that you are not alone puts fear in perspective.

- To deny fear when fear is warranted is to live foolishly.
  To deny fear when fear is warranted is to deny reality.

- To live in fear is to deny the possibilities of life.

- The denial of reality is a separation from the world.
  Separation is a cause of anxiety.
  Anxiety is one source of fear.
  Therefore, to control fear is to
  recognize reality for what it is.

- The changes of nature are inevitable.
  Accept them for what they are.

- The leaves change. The leaves fall.
  The leaves return once more.

- Everyone will know loss.
  Not to accept loss is to deny the inevitable.

- Nature has no mind; nature has no heart.
  It isn't sentimental.
  Natural disasters befall individuals
  through no fault of their own.

- To accept death is to accept humanity.

- To accept that you are human is to accept
  you are part of nature.

The Reality of Death

- You barely understand what this life is.
  How can you talk about life after death?
  Therefore, live this life well.

- Where does a wave on a lake go when the wind ceases to blow?
  Where does a cloud go when it has moved across the sky?
  That's where life goes when there is no more breath.

- I am gathered from the dust of the universe.
  I become myself when I am born.
  I become my non-self when I die.

- There was no me before my birth,
  for I am made in relation to others.
  Therefore, death is the returning to the not-me.
  I will be the not-me that existed before my birth.

- There is no me after death.
  Therefore, there is nothing to fear in death itself.
  It is a returning to the non-me.

- You are like a ripple on the water.
  You come. You go.
  You are forever.

- The great mystery is not death but that you have been born.

- The great mystery is not that those
  who have been here are now gone.
  It is that that they have been here at all.

- Let go of a past too tightly held.

- To be alone in grief is misery.
  To be with another in grief is life sanctified.

- Pain held privately is biology.
  Pain shared is a form of healing.

- Pain, while inevitable, isn't a good in and of itself.
  But pain increases the awareness of important
  things in life.

- Tragedy is unavoidable.
  You suffer fates through no fault of your own.
  Still, the sun shines and flowers bloom.

- In the face of tragedy, there is darkness and light.
  Choose light.

Changes

- Death is real; aging is real; loss is real.
  To deny reality is to live in illusion.
  Therefore, accept reality fully.
  Live the life you have been given.

- You cannot control chance; you cannot prevent tragedy.
  Hurricanes blow; seas swell high.
  Still, the sun rises and songbirds sing.

- Everything changes. Accept this and
  bend like bamboo that won't break in the wind.

- Life is bracketed by two eternities.
  On one side, the past, on the other the future.
  Today you have your name, so let us speak to one another.

- You are always in the now. Already it is gone.

- What you are doing right now is the most important thing.
  Therefore, pay attention to what you are doing.
  This may be your last moment.

- You, too, will take your place once more
  amongst the soil and the stars.

- Death is real, but no more real than love.

- Who can celebrate destruction?
  Who can dance at times of desolation?
  Look into a child's eyes and see what love there is.

- A child is born.
  A child dies.
  You are part of the natural world.

The Earth

- Celebrate the human spirit.
  Treat tenderly the earth upon which you walk.

- The body is material.
  Matter has always been and always will be.
  Therefore, only form changes.

- The proper response to nature
  is wonder, marvel and awe.

- Rock, hoe, seed —
  each a miracle, each a wonder, all sources of marvel.

- Wonder is a source of humility.
  Wisdom is always humble.

- Love the earth as your own body.
  Want for others what you desire for yourself.
  This is the way to respect.

- Can you stop a volcano from erupting?
  Then why do you think you aren't a creature of nature?

- Be open to the grandeur of nature — that is sublime.

- Celebrate the seasons.
  You, too, are transformed with the turns of the Earth.

- You are bound to this earth,
  so take time to see what is before you.
  Then your life can become a thing of beauty.

Beauty and the Heart

- Beauty is revealed when you
  learn to see with your heart.
  The more educated your heart
  the greater beauty you can see.
  Therefore, beauty is revealed with age.

- You see beauty with your heart.
  You create beauty with your actions.
  You know beauty with your mind.

- Beauty and wisdom cannot be separated.
  Beauty is the twin of joy.
  Joy is the twin of beauty.

- From a distance, everything seems beautiful.
  To see beauty in the nearby is divine.

- Look up.
  There is beauty in the sky. Look down.
  There is beauty in the earth.

- Look within.
  There is beauty in the heart. Look across from you.
  There is beauty in your neighbor's eyes.

- Some things are so beautiful that
  to hold them is to bring the sun
  to the center of the heart.
  Other things are so beautiful that
  to hold them is to die.

- Open your ears, there is beauty to be heard.
  Open your eyes, there is beauty to be seen.
  Open your heart, there is beauty to be felt.

- Walk properly upon the earth.
  Then you will know what beauty is.

- To know beauty is to know joy.
  To know joy is to know life.
  To know life is to know your connections.

- Your fate is the fate of others.
  Your fate is the fate of the Earth.
  Your fate is the fate of the stars above.

Concentric Circles

- You are neither the beginning nor the end of all things.
  You are the center of all things.

- Does the stream create itself?
  Can a person be self-created?

- Can there be waves without water?
  Can there be a self without other selves?

- To grow into your fullness is your natural goal.
  Identify with another's joys and sorrows.

- Can there be clouds without sky?
  Why do you think you can be separate
  from all other things?

- Your existence attests to mine.
  My existence attests yours.

- There is no self apart from other selves.
  You are human because you are like others.

- Your self is not a thing but a relationship.
  You are related to other things —
  people, objects and time.

- You are not separate from others.
  Therefore, to respect others is to respect yourself.

- The subject that you are is the object of others.
  You are both yourself and not yourself simultaneously.

- The present is all there is.
  The present is already gone and not-yet has become.

- You are what your eye sees
  But the eye cannot see itself.

- Only other eyes can see your eye.
  Therefore, to see yourself completely you need others.

- Reality is the flow of all relationships.
  There is no reality beyond what is.

- You are your memories and dreams.
  Therefore, honor the past by the good deeds
  you do for tomorrow.

- The present is the sum of the past and
  what you will the future to be.
  Therefore, now is the past and the future you choose

Uniqueness

- No one shares your history.
  Therefore, you are different from
  all who have ever been or ever will be.

- To deny your uniqueness is an offense against yourself.
  To find your uniqueness is a blessing.

- You are unique; you are less than perfect.
  Awareness of both preserves your humanity.

- To learn is to create.
  To create is to discover your talents.
  To discover your talents is to honor your uniqueness.
  To know that you are like others is to honor yourself.

- The self disappears when all connections dissolve.
  It is impermanent, like a ripple on the water.

- You are because of you are part of
  that which surrounds you.
  You cannot be apart from that which you are.

- You cannot be independent from your surroundings.
  You are only free to be unique.

- You are who you are because there are others.
  Without others you could not be.
  Therefore, be grateful to others for your existence.

- Be grateful for your existence.
  Repay the debt your have inherited.
  Those who are and those yet to be depend upon you.

Obligations to Others

- Do not be concerned that others haven't affirmed you.
  Be concerned that you haven't affirmed others.

- With others you share your strengths.
  From others you gain your own.

- Walk side-by-side.
  Promise to take care of one another.
  Give one another strength.
  Give one another courage to meet another day.
  This is the way of friendship.

- Seek the highest in others.
  Again and again you will create holy ground.
  It is always new and right here below your feet.

- In respecting others you find what is most precious in
  yourself.

- Friends provide light for one another.
  They accept each other not only for who they are.
  They accept each other for what they might become.

- What you say affects others.
  Therefore, you have a duty to speak truthfully and kindly.

- How you appear affects others.
  Therefore, you have an obligation to appear pleasing to
  others.

- Blame is useless.
  Not making the same mistake again is useful.

- You can't change others.
  But you can change how you react to others.

- By changing your reactions
  to others you may also change them.
  Therefore, it is possible to change others.

- To see yourself as you are, use a mirror.
  To see yourself as you might be you need a friend.

Light in a Cloud of Ignorance

- You can barely understand what thought is.
  How, then, can you talk about revelation?
  Therefore, pay attention to this world.

- Reason sheds light. Feelings radiate warmth.
  Intelligence is the sum of both.

- Knowledge is the language of the mind.
  Faith is the language of the heart.

- Mindless, heartless.
  Which is worse — starving to death or dying of thirst?

- A head full of noise cannot hear its own thoughts.

- A corrupt mind rattles with malice.
  An empty mind rattles with many words.

- The more you know the more you know
  how little you know. This is a source of humility.
  It is a source of never-ending wonder.

- Learn what to do from the wise.
  Learn what not to do from fools.
  Everyone has something to teach.

- Try to understand what can be understood.
  Reason about that which can be reasoned.

- Attempt to demonstrate what can be proven.
  Persuade others only about these things.

- Everyone has a part of the truth.
  No one has all of the truth
  Therefore, learn from everyone you meet.

- Thought influences action.
  Therefore, think clearly so that you may act thoughtfully.

- Is it possible to be thoughtful without thoughtfulness?
  Can a good person be thoughtless?

- There is no question, only questions.

- There is no answer, only answers.

There is always a Choice

- That which interferes with sound
judgment needs to be rectified.

- Someone made the wrong choice and died.
Someone refused to choose and someone else died.
Someone made the right choice and died happy.

- Every choice opens possibilities.
Every choice closes possibilities.

- Choosing presents risks.
Not choosing presents risks.

- There are limits imposed by the natural world.
There are limits imposed by human nature.
There are limits imposed by your own nature.
There are limits imposed by the times in which you live.
Accept with equanimity the things that cannot change.

- There are limits you impose upon yourself.
There are limits you impose upon others.
Such limits may be either good or bad.
Learn to know the difference.

- Everyone has limitations.
Not to accept your limitations is to know frustration.

- No life turns out as planned.
Therefore, don't be attached to expectations.
There are always new choices to be made.

- Can one rabbit run for another?
Can one bird sing for another?
Then how can one person think for another?

- Make a space in which to think.
Make a place in which to feel.

- Take the time to know where you are.
Take the time to choose wisely.

Choosing the Good

- The hat doesn't fit.
  Do you change the head or the hat?

- It is better not to injure than it is to do harm.
  It is better to do good than to do no harm.

- Goodness is bringing out the best in others.

- Bring out the best in others and
  you bring out the best in yourself.

- Do good and you will become good.

- The good you look for is more important
  than the bad you find.

- Don't wait for proof of goodness.
  Act as though it is there and help create it.

- Never make less of yourself than you are.
  Never think you are more than another.

- Good thoughts by themselves do not make life good.

- Good feelings by themselves do not make life good.
  A person who does good is good.

- To be full of heart but not do good is to be not good.
  It is how the heart is used that matters.

- No one is perfect.
  Aim to repair the hurt you have caused.
  Do less harm in the future.

- A good life is the flourishing of human activity.
  Cultivate your abilities.
  Allow others to cultivate theirs.

- It is better to be good than right.

- It is better to do good than to feel good.

- Nothing is perfect.
  Still, there is goodness to be had.

Creating the Good

- What you say creates the world in which you live.
  A better world is achieved in the process of right speech.

- What you think creates the world in which yo u live.
  A better world is achieved by right thought.

- What you think you see creates
  the world in which you live.
  See the goodness in the world and
  you will create a good world.

- Within the best is some bad.
  Within the worst is some good.
  Acknowledging both leads to a better world.

- Don't let the bad you see convince you
  that people are nothing but evil.
  Don't let the evil you see convince you
  that the world is nothing but bad.
  See the reality that is beyond appearances.

- Cultivate the good, but pay attention to the bad,
  You contain parts that are less than good.
  What you won't acknowledge will harm you.

- Beware of self-righteousness.
  It is a great pitfall of those who aspire to goodness.

- Cultivate humility.
  It is the way of solidarity.

- Beware of false humility —
  It leads to self-righteousness.

- Pride is necessary.
  Misplaced pride is dangerous.

- When you see yourself too grandly,
  you cannot truly know the world.
  It is like trying to touch an object in a mirror.

- The challenge of the young is to develop humility.
  The challenge of the old is to maintain hope.

- Be skeptical of purity.
  Admit that you don't have all the answers.

- Each is born with unique endowments.
  Each is born in a certain place.
  Therefore, be humble.

- Each is born at a particular time.
  All are born with limited endowments.
  There, your achievements aren't yours alone.

- Some are born in places of misfortune.
  Some are born in times of calamity.
  Therefore, be generous in your judgment of others.

- Make a space in which to think.
  Make a place in which to feel.
  Take the time to know where you are.
  Take the time to know who you are.

- Pay attention. Stay awake.
  For the moment lay aside all ambition.
  For the moment set aside all plans.

- A clenched hand leads to a lonely life.
  A lonely life cannot be a happy life.
  Therefore, open your hand and give what you are able.

When your heart
has been opened
happiness is infinite

A Generous Spirit

- Generosity of spirit creates a life worth living.

- Never promote yourself at another's expense.

- A thoughtful person thinks for herself.
  A thoughtless person thinks only of herself.

- Is it possible to be a thoughtful person without thoughtfulness? Can a good person be thoughtless?

- Allow each person the dignity of his or her own labor.

- Wealth justly gained is honorable.
  Wealth unjustly gained is disgraceful.
  Wealth kept for one's self is shameful.

- Owning things isn't bad.
  Being owned by things is bad.

- Goodness is a gift from those who went before.
  Therefore, make things better for those who come after.

Children

- Cupped hands hold water.
  Open arms hold love.
  With your eyes you show admiration.
  With your breath you give life.

- Good children need good homes.
  Good homes need good times.
  Good times need good governments.

- Good governments require just people.
  Just people are those who have been educated properly.

- Children need adults for protection.
  Adults need elders for wisdom.
  Elders need children for hope.

- If you grow old well, you will grow young again.

- Children call attention to themselves.
  Adults pay attention to others.

- Children think they know everything.
  Adults know how little they know.

- As a child, walk. As an adult, work.
  As an old person, act wisely.

- A child is not born with a corrupt nature.
  A child is not born with a good nature.
  A child's nature is both.

- It is better to elicit goodness than
  it is to beat out badness.
  When goodness is brought out,
  someone becomes good.
  When badness is beaten out,
  someone lives in shame.
  Goodness is elicited with respect and love.

Love and Hate

- You love — who knows why?
  You know joy — does the reason matter?
  There is kindness — what love!
  What joy!

- Love with an educated heart.

- What does love mean if you hug too tightly?

- What does love mean if the other isn't cherished?

- What does love mean without doing what love requires?

- In love the ordinary is made sacred.

- Some fires consume in a flash.
  Others smolder forever
  Which is the greater love?

- Love can never be learned alone.
  It always requires a teacher.

- When love is learned well,
  life is filled with beauty.

- When the heart is full of hatred,
  you will know only ugliness.

- To hate what is hateful is to love what is good.
  Better than hating what is hateful is doing what is good.

- Non-hatred is good.
  Respect is better.

Respect

- There can be no respect without self-respect.
  There can be no self-respect without respecting others.

- Respect honors the uniqueness of each person.

- Nourish, encourage, cooperate —
  These are the ways to respect.

- Honesty, kindness, respect —
  These are the paths to the sacred.

- When you value the important things,
  you respect yourself.

- Resentment hinders self-respect.
  Therefore, self-respect requires
  quieting the fires of resentment.

- Before forgiveness can be accepted
  there must contrition.

- If the offense is petty,
  forgive without payment.

- If the offense is great,
  there must be restitution.

- Here are the sources of self-respect:
  Hold yourself to your highest self.
  Accept responsibility for yourself.
  Accept responsibility for the larger world.

Less than Perfect

- Self-delusion is helpful, in small measure.
  Self-doubt is useful, in small measure.

- Inconsistency is desirable, in small measure.
  Accept imperfections, in small measure.

- Don't pursue the perfect.
  Cultivate the human instead.

- You cannot know everything that is knowable.
  Accept that your knowledge is incomplete.

- You cannot see everything because
  you cannot see everywhere.
  Accept that your perceptions are partial.

- In a desert, a tree offers shade.
  In a forest, an opening offers sunshine.

- In a drought you say, Rain, rain.
  In a storm you say, Sun, sun.

- Tears — water in which to drown
  or rain to quench the spirit?

- Is water the same once it has fallen?
  Are rains and rivers the same?

- The door is open.
  Has someone gone or is someone coming in?

- You cannot know about life before this life.
  You cannot know about life beyond this life.
  Therefore, cultivate the best in this life.

The Body

- Not to enjoy what nature has given
  you is an offence against yourself.

- Your senses take you here.
  Therefore, you can love what is around you.

- Your imagination can take you there.
  Therefore, you can love what you have
  never known before.

- Food is both a necessity and a pleasure.
  So eat in ways that are both healthy and enjoyable.

- Food is a gift of nature.
  All gifts should honor the gift-giver.

- Be grateful for the food you eat.
  Remember those who do not have enough to eat.

- Pleasures of the body are one of the joys of life.
  Too much pleasure makes you dull.

- Dullness interferes with good judgment.
  Poor judgment impedes future pleasures.

- Too little pleasure and you die of thirst.
  Too much pleasure and you drown.

- Keep still — that is the sun you feel.
  Keep still — that is the taste of pollen on your tongue.
  Keep still — that is life that you smell.
  Keep still — that is love that you see.

- To experience pleasure is a gift of life.
  To deny pleasure is to dishonor life.

- The greatest pleasure comes from doing the right thing.
  The right thing comes from a generous heart
  and a thoughtful mind.

- Your ears are yours alone.
  Tell others what you alone can hear.

- Your voice is yours alone.
  Tell others what only you can say.

- Your eyes are yours alone.
  Show others what only you can see.

- Take care of yourself. Let the world in.

The Self

- What you are doing right now is the most important thing.
  This, too, is a moment of beauty.

- You can barely understand what a dream is.
  How, then, can you talk about visions?

- If there is another reality, it will care for itself.
  Only you can care for the life you are now living.

- The self is at the center of life's circle.
  Moments of solitude and quiet make
  clearer the nature of that self.

- In silence you hear the essence of things.
  In silence you hear your own being.

- To live with all motion is to live as though with no sense.
  Learn to keep still — that is the butterfly you hear.

- Silence helps to restore you to yourself.

- Silence is a doorway to the sacred.
  It is a tool for self-knowledge.

- The wisdom of the past and the dreams of the future are
  eternal. They stand here in the timeless present of quiet
  reflection.

- Learn from others what is good.
  Examine yourself for what is bad.

- Gratitude restores you to yourself.
  In gratitude you can witness the miracle of being.

- Be grateful for that which you share with others.
  Remember those who suffer from loneliness.

- Others have a rightful claim on you.
  Therefore, measure your pleasures and
  gains against others.

- Today is full of the past.
  The present is pregnant with the future.

- Be thankful for what you have inherited.
  You are responsible to use it wisely.

The Miraculous

- "Where did I come from?" someone once asked.
  "I don't know," was the answer.

- "Where will I go when I'm no longer here?" someone once
  asked. "Where you once came from," was the answer.

- "What should I do while I am here?" someone once asked.
  The answer was, "Find the miraculous in your neighbor."

- Some think nothing is sacred, some think everything is.
  The sacred isn't a place to be discovered.
  But is a condition that is created in acts of loving-kindness.

- Within each person is a seed of genius.
  With right relations it will flower.

- Hold life as sacred. Treat it with reverence.

- Act with care.
  Act with respect.

- Work that does no harm is honorable work.
  Work that contributes to humanity is noble work.

- You are successful when others benefit from your efforts.
  You are unsuccessful when others are diminished by what
  you do.

- Gardeners must care for their gardens.
  Since you live in others' gardens you must
  care for others, too.

- Some plants bloom best when pot bound.
  Some die unless wild.

- To touch is to admit that something else exists.
  To be touched is to know that you exist.
  To exist is a miracle.

- Some plants thrive in dappled light.
  Some need direct sunlight.
  Every plant needs proper soil.

- The proper soil for human cultivation is respect.
  From respect grows the miracle of love

State of Grace

- Live life compassionately.

- Live life fully.

- Live life responsibly.

- Live life thoughtfully.

- Live life full of wonder.

- Here are two major stances towards life:
  Live your life full of grace.
  Live your life full of dignity.

- Grace is achieved when you feel yourself as part of what is.
  Therefore, accept the wonder of the world.

- Dignity is achieved when you accept the dignity of others.
  Therefore, live responsibly as part of the social world.

- Happiness is achieved when you live with grace and dignity.

- Disgrace is separating yourself
  from that to which you belong.
  Not honoring that which deserves
  to be honored is a disgrace.

- To act honorably is to act justly.
  Give everyone his or her due.

- Honor those who have gone before.
  To honor the past is to endow the future.

- The honorable person is mindful of the world.
  Peace of heart cannot be taken from the honorable person.

- A peaceful heart is an accepting heart.
  Accept yourself as you might become.

- An accepting heart accepts others' shortcomings.

- Accept the changes nature brings.
  Winter, too, is beautiful.

- When a butterfly flutters in China,
  it will rain next week in California.
  So why do you think that what you do doesn't matter?

- It is the little heroes who, in the long run,
  make the difference.

The Great Questions

- "Is there life after death?" someone wanted to know.
  This is the wrong question.
  The appropriate question is "How do I best live my life?"

- "Is there a God?"
  This also is the wrong question.
  The appropriate question is:
  "How do I live my life as though each
  contains a spark of the divine?"

- "Is there heaven?" someone wanted to know.
  This is the wrong question.
  The appropriate question is
  "How can I make heaven a reality?"

- The great questions aren't about life somewhere else.
  They are not about life sometime else.
  The great questions are about here, now.

- The question isn't "Who is God?"
  The question is "Who am I?"

- The question isn't "What does God mean?"
  The question is "What does being human mean?"

- When the chain of goodness is broken,
  how should you live? Do your part to repair the break.

- When your heart is breaking, where do you find solace?
  By honoring those who are no longer with you.

- How do you honor those who are no longer with you?
  By embodying their best in your own life.

- Be honest with yourself:
  What do you refuse to see?

- Be honest with yourself.
  What do you refuse to ask?

- Be honest with yourself.
  What do you refuse to listen to?

- Question yourself. Change the world.

CPSIA information can be obtained
at www.ICGtesting.com
Printed in the USA
LVHW051314210121
677073LV00008B/303